The Unknown Power
The New Believer's Guide to Non-Religious Faith

ISBN: 978-1-944901-34-9

Copyright © 2025 by Speaking Freedom LLC
All rights reserved.
No portion of this book may be reproduced without written permission from the publisher or author, except as permitted by U.S. copyright law.

Book Cover by: Kaci Winslow

Publisher Website: speakingfreedom.org

Other Website Information: SpeakingfreedomTV.org, edu-freedom.org

Publisher Address: 75 Washington St. #1177, Fairburn, GA 30213

Speaking Freedom Books' Disclaimers

Welcome to Speaking Freedom Books, which provides advanced spiritual study and personal development insights. We thank you for your purchase and look forward to helping you grow in all areas of your life.

God bless.

Please listen clearly to all disclaimers provided. If you are currently under a physician's care, please maintain that relationship.

Please note that all results are based on the individual's ability to adapt and adjust to any given environment and situation. The life-enhancement coaches at Speaking Freedom provide information to help you grow. You are responsible for maintaining that growth and applying the information to your individual life.

This book was written by Speaking Freedom Books, Concept by Kaci (Winslow) Myers.

For best results, you will need an open mind, the ability to research, and a balanced lifestyle.

Table of Contents

The Introduction

Chapter 1: Maturity Levels of Believers

Chapter 2: Understanding Faith
    What Faith Is
    What Faith is Not
    Child-Like Faith,
    Doing is Better Than Believing,
    Actions More Powerful Than Words,
    Faith Without Works Explained

Chapter 3: How God Speaks (Overview)

Chapter 4: Self-Knowledge is God Knowledge

Chapter 5: Lessons of No Results

Chapter 6: Small Results, Big Effects

Chapter 7: Learn History

Afterthoughts & Words from Xavier & Nya Myers

Introduction.

This book is designed for the individual who desires to grow spiritually, for the new believer who is seeking to grow, know, and advance in faith, for the spiritually awakened who is seeking to deepen their relationship with God and depend on only faith, and for the seasoned believer looking to see God's new wave, how God speaks today, and how to move forward efficiently.

The message intended with this book is that it does not take many years of faith to receive God's favor but that your level of faith is based on your level of belief. And the more you believe, the bigger your favor and faith will be. We will also introduce a new term and hope to establish a new field in psychology.

Spiritual human behavior represents the spiritual aspect of all human behavior and how life shaped you for your purpose.

Knowing your heritage and background, as well as understanding the reasons behind your beliefs, is significant.

These key things will help you grow in knowledge, wisdom, and understanding and establish your faith with great confidence, leadership, and the ability to garner the favor you need to make your dreams a reality.

For a more detailed guide to applying faith to your individual life, you can purchase The Faith Collection, a step-by-step personal faith guide consisting of four individual books on faith: Faith 101: The Basics, Faith 201: The Great Awakening of Calculated Moves, Faith 301: The Results of Self Love, and Faith 401: Faith Cultivated Love.

This series builds on what you learn in The Unkn Power.

"Spiritual Human Behavior" is also available to help you understand the psychology of who you are and how to fulfill your purpose!

Chapter 1: Maturity Levels of Believers

There are many maturity levels associated with being a believer. Below are the four most common, often seen in churches and other religious settings. The maturity levels described are inconclusive and are not always based on age. People start their spiritual journey at different ages, so spiritual maturity varies from person to person and from culture to culture. This is a brief overview of the four common maturity levels and brief descriptions corresponding to each level.

Don't think of a believer in the religious sense when you think of a believer. Think of someone who believes in God (The Universe) and has faith in something bigger than themselves.

Maturity Levels Defined

The first level of a believer is *The Seasoned Believer*.

The Seasoned Believer has been believing for a very long time and has achieved many results while struggling with fear but knows how to navigate for the most part. Their accomplishments often fall short of their full potential but represent what they have felt comfortable with due to the fear of failure. Seasoned Believers can hide their struggles with overzealous behaviors masking fear, doubt, timidity, and similar emotions. They are likely to express doubt and fear based on their strongholds to others, often against any progress in understanding God. They are known to judge spirituality outside their knowledge and understanding realm.

The next level of Believers is *The Mature Believer*.

The Mature Believers are still fresh in their faith. They still believe like a baby or new believer with Child-Like Faith, but they have had some victories that strengthen their ability to receive. Mature Believers are often seen as rebels because they obtain new-age spiritual beliefs without excessive fear. They can also combat and stand for what they believe in against the older, "seasoned" believers who tend to talk people out of what they truly believe God can do through them.

The next level of Believer is *The Baby and New Believer*.

They are considered The Baby Believers or New Believers because their faith remains Child-Like, as it is fresh. They haven't experienced enough hardship to tarnish their faith and belief in God. New Believers are more likely to be unsure whether something is of God or Not, which can lead them to seek mentorship or guidance from an experienced believer. When you have Child-Like Faith, you are eager to believe in what God says and confirms. Believers with this level of spiritual maturity are highly impressionable and strongly desire to please God (The Universe). They believe all things are possible, so they can overcome and achieve more things in life because their faith hasn't been broken.

The last level of Believers is *The Elder*.

When you think of an elder, you're thinking of someone who is older, someone who has been a part of a church or a religious establishment for a very long time.

Honestly, an Elder is a person who is experienced in their faith, someone who has personally experienced God, someone who knows who God is and knows how God speaks. There are times when Elders can be older people in a church or older believers. This book isn't about religion or the church; it's about learning how to cultivate your faith, understanding your place within it, and knowing how to proceed and thrive based on faith, not religion. The elders are the people who have normally experienced more, grown more and won more spiritual battles.

Every now and then, you will find people who deem themselves Elders, but they haven't had the experience of wins and results that caused them to be Elders. Some Elders are open to what God is doing in the present day while honoring who God has been and the evolution of the spiritual walk in modern times. While others are not budging from the old way of doing things. The latter of the two have been trusting God for a very long time, but they have varying results or no results.

Results are an important part of being a believer. Many can claim to be believers, but if they don't have the results to demonstrate how their belief pattern is effective, then they must examine where their faith and belief have a disconnect.

Elders have a responsibility to examine and dissect what it means to be an elder, while others explore how to become one and grow so that others can be encouraged, strengthened, and move forward.

How it Works Together

When Elders understand how they've learned to move forward, people imitating their faith becomes the purpose and reason why they are there. Elders should help young believers grow into stronger believers and become more faithful providing knowledge and understanding of God. There are levels and layers to almost everything, not just being a believer, but we'll start with that here.

As you continue to read the series of books, you'll be able to understand precisely what it means to have different levels and layers. When you think of an elder, you encounter two distinct levels and layers. One has learned, gotten the results, and is experienced, but may not be old.

There is also the older believer who may not have achieved results, who may not have experienced the type of triumphs that would genuinely make them an elder, trusted with younger followers or newer believers who need guidance, a mentor, or even help to secure and grow their faith.

With the more mature Spiritual Elder, you have those who have learned to lean on God, pray to God, and cultivate a deep intimacy with God, regardless of their religious affiliation. On the other hand, you have those who talk a lot, who haven't experienced much to exercise their faith, but they're old.

Older people, in general, feel that they should have some say in what goes on within the younger generation of believers. The last of the two are the ones that generally fill young believers with doubt. Often, they've had more defeats than victories, although sometimes their concerns are warranted, as they've also witnessed the events that have shaped their perspective on the world around them.

They may not have had things go their way, seen other people suffer, or may not have received the things they've prayed for. When young, fresh, new believers believe all things are possible or that anything can be attained, the way the Bible talks about it, the Older Elders that haven't experienced that will tell you to stay within the circle of comfort of things that we think that you can accomplish or you can do based on how we've learned to believe.

The Elders aren't always the best to teach you how to believe in God for the impossible. Sometimes, they haven't learned the proper way to think from the beginning, so it's hard for them to tell, show, instruct, or help you to enhance how you believe if you're a new believer or even if you're a mature believer. That's why learning whose faith to imitate is so essential when based on results.

So many people think because you're around someone who has been believing, been saved, or whatever you want to call it for so long, they can teach you a lot. But if they haven't learned how to win, implement, and apply the knowledge, skills, wisdom, discernment, and all the things that come with truly having faith in God (The Universe) as a source, then how helpful can they be? They won't be able to tell, help, or show you how to mature as a believer in the correct way unless they guide you from lessons they've learned from their own life experiences.

The more you try to receive things by faith, and it doesn't happen, the more you tarnish your ability to believe if you hold on to the doubt.

Not all older or mature believers hold onto doubt. However, there are a large number of people who have been in faith for many years and still have not experienced the true fullness of God.

They may get blessed here and there sporadically, but I'm talking about on purpose. When you win on purpose, it creates a different reality. Every time you know *how* to win, it's a matter of knowing the formula or step-by-step process. You know how to recreate whatever it is that you're trying to receive, starting in your mind first and then allowing God to guide you into manifesting it into your life.

So, what makes an elder? An elder is someone who knows how to speak directly to God about their concerns and knows how to listen for answers. What an elder is not is someone who demands, points fingers, and judges everyone who achieves results different from their own.

 It is essential to note that we are not attempting to shame or downplay any older generation. The fact remains that being older doesn't necessarily make you an experienced or knowledgeable believer. I've personally known people 60 and 70 years old who still struggle day to day with faith, trusting God, and healing from their childhood trauma.

They're still calling TV prayer lines, thinking they'll get results without any corresponding action. They may or may not receive the result, but they lack faith in their personal relationship with God. One of the best things about growing in faith is learning to have a personal relationship with God for yourself, by yourself, so that everything outside of your relationship with God is supplemental; it adds to it and enhances it.

Nothing outside of yourself can hurt, harm, diminish, or minimize your personal relationship and connection with God as your source. Many people who have been believing for a long time tie it to religion. What I've learned through my studies and personal experience is that religion wasn't the origin of God.

Religion was an extension and expression of one person's account of God. What they experienced, and what they told other people as witnesses. They were not giving you a step-by-step guide but instead showing you how God works and the start of possibilities. Showing the type of results that come from being one with God and following his instructions for you, especially for leaders. It outlines how God communicates and how to foster that relationship despite challenges or opposition.

Side Note: From what we can gather from the Bible and other sacred texts, it appears that God speaks to some but not all, and there is no discernible reason why God chooses any person.

What we find is that elders can become bossy because they've become so accustomed to their ways and traditions that they hinder growth in some people. Sometimes, controlling personality traits can stem from not feeling like you have control over your own life, so you control others. This doesn't apply to everybody because not everyone views elders in the same way.

Every account for an elder will be unique. Someone else might view an elder as an older person and assume that, simply because they're old, they must know everything. However, sometimes older people are more inexperienced than those who are newer to faith, those who are eager to believe in God and have never been tainted.

We're not religious here at Speaking Freedom, although Love Gang is a Non-Religious Community for Believers. The Bible and other sources of information that many people rely on for health, wholeness, and a sound mind are referenced through our library of titles.

I will warn you that we may not always be politically correct. Still, we will always be honest, open, and transparent about what we've experienced and know and how to implement great things into your own lives to help you grow along with us.

Let's discuss The Seasoned Believers and The Experienced Believers.

We strive to ensure that every level of believer can achieve the same powerful results. It's a matter of holding onto your faith, not allowing discouragement, resentment, past failures, or anything else to get in the way of believing God for new things to come into your life.

Here are a few more things about the Seasoned Believer, and then we'll move on to the Mature Believers. Mature believers, if they have attained the promises of God in their lives, will be God-seeing. This means they see with the eyes of God.

They will teach you how to believe, and they will help you stay focused on what you believe, not on what you desire, but on what

God desires for you. That is key. If you focus solely on your prayers on what you think you want rather than on what God desires, you will come to doubt, experience resentment, and become unbelieving because you're not understanding or praying for what God wants for you.

This makes you less likely to see exactly what you want or God's best because you're praying for what you think you deserve, and God usually thinks you deserve more. The experienced believer who has learned how to walk by faith, not by sight, who has learned to trust God for not what they want but for what God wants for them, knowing that whatever God has for them will be the desires of their heart and what God has purpose for them within their soul purpose. They're more likely to receive what they need, want, and desire simply by living on faith.

The best part about an experienced believer should be their ability to positively impact the youth of believers, those who look up to them, and those who need guidance. If you're unable to help them grow in every area of their life, then you may need to experience God more deeply to be the Experienced, Seasoned Believer that a Baby Believer needs to help them grow.

So, your next question, I'm sure, is: What is a mature believer?

A mature believer is someone who is fine-tuned or has begun to fine-tune where they are in God, how they've gotten to a point of not being a babe because they know what steps to take, what works and how to combat and fight off all of the things that used to get them off, make them scared or fearful when they were just a baby believer.

It's very common to be a mature believer, someone who has made changes in their life, grown spiritually and mentally, and implemented practices that have allowed them to flourish both spiritually and naturally. That's very important. When thinking of a mature believer, you're referring to a person who still possesses a childlike faith; they still have the ability to recognize the real issues in life and address them.

They are very aware and conscious of the world around them and aren't afraid to beat the odds. They are often very resilient and strong. They do what they have to do because they are aware of God's promises.

They're still in a place where they pray for God's answers, not their own. They pray for God's vision, not their own. The cornerstone of their faith is prayer and follow-through.

Being a mature believer means that you have a well-rounded view of how to win with God, how to move forward with God, and how to get results. The difference between a Mature Believer and an Elder Believer is not a matter of time but accountability, responsibility, and self-discipline. You can be a mature elder and know how to win, but being an "elder" doesn't necessarily make you Mature.

Over time, they'll have fewer errors and bloopers. You don't make the same mistakes that some seasoned elders with doubts may make on small things. The difference between the seasoned and the mature can be as simple as allowing belief and faith to evolve.

It's less pressure not being considered an Elder, as you are not placed under the same pressure to be an example, to be everything a young believer should aspire to be. Elders are supposed to be the backbone of the faith and wisdom of the belief system. The babies can see from the mature people how they have evolved and grown from being babies into mature individuals.

With mature believers, there will be a fine line between them and the elders. It's a more distinct line between the mature believers and the babes because the mature believers are those individuals who are strong enough to overcome the things that the babes need much guidance on. Although babes need guidance, there is power in being fresh as a New Believer.

When you talk about the mature believer and the elder, it's almost like a fine line, and it will be the same when you're talking about the babe believer. However, the difference between the New Believer, the mature believer, and the elder is experience. With a New Believer, you're going to see something so fresh as they believe that all things are possible.

They haven't experienced enough of anything in their belief system regarding their new spiritual journey with God (The Universe) to have doubts. They haven't had enough experience to have the timidity that an older person may have. All they have is Child Like Faith, which we will explore in more detail next.

When you think of a child and their faith, consider that if you tell a child something, they believe you because they have no reason to doubt. The only question a child will have is, when will it happen? How will it happen? And are we there yet? Is it happening yet? Is it time yet? And that's the importance of childlike faith.

As we build, you will understand what it means to be a babe and what makes them powerful. Inexperience is what truly makes them powerful, as they lack doubt. They don't have anything that makes them sway in their minds, thinking, ' Will it happen? ' How, or is God capable of doing it? All they know is that they prayed, they believe, they may need to get instruction, and then they'll receive.

That's the most powerful part about being a New believer: they are inexperienced and only know what has been told to them. They know what to believe based on their communication patterns with God, their spiritual mentor or leader, or their upbringing and experiences, and they've achieved victories in their own lives.

Even when I first started experiencing victories, it wasn't in church. I wasn't taught to worship God in the way tradition dictates. I was experiencing God based on my sense of self, what I knew to be true about me, and what I wanted to experience in my life. Of course, I have dreams and visions and other things that helped me to be closer to God and walk this path with God.

However, that's an experience that everyone must have for themselves. If you're able to have visions and dreams, I tell you, believe them, trust them, and go towards what you've seen in your dreams and your visions. It will lead you to the perfect place that God has for you; everything that you could ever want need, desire, or hope for is on that path.

Chapter 2: Understanding Faith

What Faith is

Let me explain what faith is. Faith is the ability to believe in the unseen until it is manifested.

In layperson's terms, that means faith is knowing something can be yours, doing the work to get it, and having the evidence that one day, in time, you will receive what it is that you believe in. I know that may seem deep or illogical, but if you think about anything in life that you've hoped, desired, wished, or prayed for since childhood, it took faith to achieve it. It's an uncommon belief in the possibilities.

It takes faith to pray to God and trust for a response of any sort.

It even takes faith not to believe or to be an atheist. You have to have faith that nothing else exists, even to believe that nothing exists. Whether you believe in God or you're an atheist, it still takes faith to hold your ground on whatever you believe.

So you want a new car. It takes faith to secure a job and earn the money to buy that car. You want a new house and to finance the home.

It takes faith to get your paperwork together, to walk into a lender or a home builder and say, ' Here's my paperwork.' I want this house. What does it take for me to get it? Faith is not what is actually received but the belief that leads to receiving.

What you receive in the end is a result of faith.

The byproduct of faith. Faith is believing that it can happen before it's any evidence, before you can see it, and before you know how it's going to happen.

Faith is saying, " You know what? I want it. I see it in my mind, and I'll get it. I don't know how it will happen. I don't know when it will happen, but I know it will happen." Working towards all the things you need to do actually to obtain that.

Let's dive further into Child Like Faith.

As I discussed before, if you think about children and how they believe whatever their parent tells them until their parent is dishonest or untruthful, a child will continue to believe whatever you say until you have been proven to be something other than the truth.

To have childlike faith is to believe despite what you see, no matter what is presented before you, when you can't see and don't know how it's going to happen. Still, you pray and ask God, Buddha, or quote The Prophet Muhammad, or whichever spiritual culture you gravitate towards. You may or may not pray or believe in God. No matter what you believe or don't believe, whatever is planned to happen in your life will happen.

It still takes a childlike faith because children aren't aware of religious limitations without being taught it. Children only know that if their parents say it, that it will happen. That's the same type of faith that believers should have at every maturity level when it comes to faith in God. Having a strong belief or faith that, no matter what you see, desire, pray about, or hope for from God, it will eventually come to pass.

If you're a person who doesn't believe in God, it still takes faith to get up every day, be confident in going against 95% of the earth's population, and still get up to live your best life.

Religion causes people to go against God because they don't like the rules, idolization, and idolatry that come with it. In some ways, I honestly understand because I don't believe in religion. I had my time; I spent six years deeply involved in the church, and I was probably the most religious person you've ever known.

If you weren't doing things the exact way my religious beliefs stated then you had to be away from me. However, it wasn't based on my personal experience with God or what I knew to be accurate; it was based on religious principles.

With faith, everything that God wants for you is not always going to be in that book. And people may not want to hear this, but God is greater than the Bible. The Bible discusses the "greater works" that we are to do because we believe in God and Christ because of their faith and love that works in them. Your faith should be in God. God is Love.

Love births you, and gives you purpose and hope.

Love instills a twinkling feeling in your heart that says there's more to life than this. It doesn't take religion to know God. Religion can be a great starting point for some, but that's not the path God has for everyone, and it isn't the totality of God.

We live in a very religious culture and society, a world deeply rooted in religion. We are made to believe it is going to be difficult for some to navigate within God without religion. However, in my own assessment, I learned that sometimes you have to delve deeply into religion and learning. When you balance and become exactly who God called you to be you will realize that God didn't create you to be overly complex. God created you to be human.

God created you to be loved. God created you to be a friend. God created you to be more than what you see physically. To be the spiritual being that he placed within you with purpose, a calling, a gift, and so much to give into the people's lives that you're able to touch on a day-to-day basis, you will need to master faith.

What Faith is Not

Let me tell you what faith is not since we've touched on what faith is. Faith is not always the safest course of action. Sometimes, faith requires courage, and that's why you must have faith in the things you cannot see because sometimes you won't see what God is doing next.

Sometimes, you have to take the step.

Faith is not safe, even when cautious of real consequences.

Faith is not fearful, timid, or cautious because of false evidence appearing real. Faith is guided and led. Faith is walking a path that you know you can trust and believe in, knowing that whatever happens on that path is what was meant to be. It guides you to where faith is leading you and to where God has planned for you.

Some people may disagree with how you exercise your faith, but as long as you are not doing anything morally, ethically, or just plain against God, then go get your blessings.

That's not what I'm here for. I am here to help ignite and support your faith, as far as it is allowed or able to grow. However, your faith is only stopped, halted, or tarnished by your own belief system, by what you allow into yourself because what you allow in is what eventually comes out.

Child Like Faith

Let's talk more about childlike faith because if you think about the way a child is born into this world, they are solely dependent on their parents or whoever their guardian is if they're not with their parents.

This is the way we have to rely on God or the source that we individually depend on. Everyone doesn't believe in God; as I discussed before, we're not here to specify who you should believe in, but that you believe in a greater source overseeing the Universe and earth. Sometimes, that greater source is within and not without, and your childlike faith should exemplify that. It should show exactly how you believe what you believe; sometimes, it's blind faith because children don't know any better.

Children do not understand concepts like money, homes, or lack of possessions. Children often don't know how to distinguish between what they are told and what is true. All they know is to believe, and that's where we want you to be as a new believer.

That's the power of being a new believer: the fact that you haven't been tainted, you only trust God, and you only see and hear what God is sharing and telling you, as long as you don't have anyone else in your ear telling you the opposite.

Just as with children, you must monitor what you allow them to watch, eat, be around, and hear. You have to monitor everything that a child does so that you can ensure that they're going on the path that you desire them to be, a strong path, somewhere where they'll be fearless, respectful, feel guided, and know that they have your comfort, they're loved, that everything that they need. They can always depend on and rely on you to supply their needs.

That is the relationship that we should have with God, the creator and our source for everything.

Doing Better Than Believing

The reason *doing is better than only believing* is that you can believe many things, but if you don't put actions behind what you believe, then believing alone won't yield the results you're hoping for.

We believe in God.

Yes, but what do you do to show you believe in God? For me, it's prayer and meditation. It's the ability to get to know what God sounds like, who God is, and how God moves.

This can be achieved in various ways. Most people turn to the Bible to gain a deeper understanding of God. That's what I recommend the Bible for, not as a guide and a map to exactly how you should do it. I see the Bible as something that has been created to give you a testimony and an account of how God has moved in the past, what God is like, and how God speaks to you.

Not necessarily that God will say exactly what's been said in the Bible, or that he will have you doing exactly what's already in the Bible, but that's where it's good to have individuals in your lives that have testimony and can tell you exactly how God has moved in them, with them and through them. Often, we have an imaginary type of belief system where we think that merely believing is enough, but it is not. Some people believe that they will never see the promises of God or the fullness of God. Some will only believe enough to get into heaven. If you believe that believing itself is the only thing you need to get into heaven, then go ahead and believe; however, let's examine this further.

What if we are supposed to create a heaven here on earth as we live, and then we are birthed from death into another lifetime? Believing is good, but what did God place you on this earth to live for? What did God place you here to do?

There are things that God placed you on this planet to accomplish in your life. But if you're only believing, you'll never even believe enough to ask God, what am I supposed to do?

Actions are More Powerful Than Words

When you think about the Bible or any book that offers knowledge, wisdom, and guidance, simply having the book itself is insufficient.

To know itself means nothing if you're not applying the knowledge to your everyday life. So yes, we want you to know things. We want you to be familiar with things, have a sense of awareness, and be acquainted with things. Most of all, you have to be able to do something with what you know. Just knowing by itself means nothing and defeats the purpose because having knowledge that you cannot use is a waste of time.

So how do you decide what to do after you believe? Well, first, pray.

Don't only pray, "Hallowed be thy name, thy kingdom come, thy will be done on earth as it is in heaven." Yes, that's a portion of it. But ask God specifically, what does he have for your life? What is the will of God for your life? How to walk out the purpose of God for your life? Then, ask for the strength to carry out each and everything that God has already set in the line for your life.

There is a path that God placed you on earth to take. How do you go about taking it? You can't just believe that there is a path and not take it. Well, you can, but if you're going to believe that there is a path and a purpose from God for your life, my suggestion is that you take it. Seek God for the answers so that you know how to accomplish what you were placed on earth for.

So, what exactly do you believe, and how do you plan to walk out and see what you're believing in or what you truly believe? You believe in God; how do you show it? You believe that you will be someone great. What type of greatness are you believing for? What will you do to reach that greatness? For all we know, some people could be placed on earth not to believe so that they can learn to trust in God for themselves, by themselves, with no assisted help. No tradition, no religion, nothing.

So that God can prove himself to them in their lives. What we do know is that everybody has a purpose. Finding that purpose for each and every person may be a challenge for some, but that's where we come in. We help you discover your purpose, teaching you not only how to believe in and practice faith, but also how to cultivate it. Speaking Freedom is also committed to helping you live out the faith you have and for which you have faith because there's no point in having faith in something and then not doing anything with it.

Going to school to learn about something and then not applying that knowledge is a waste of money, time, and mental energy. The goal is to apply what you know to your life.

In a society where words are cheap, everyone can express their beliefs and share their thoughts. Everyone can say a lot of things, but how many do what they say they believe, how they say they believe it, and then can show you how to do it yourself and get results?

What is the point of knowing something if you're not able to help, teach, share, and instruct others on how to either do it or how to be greater than you at it? The true test of who you are as a leader and as a person is how you lead and guide others to being great or even greater than yourself. It's more of a testament to the person who's already in a position. If the people that are under them come and become greater than them, then it is to say how great they are. Who have you helped become greater? Whom have you shown how to do what you know? That's a part of doing better than just believing.

I can believe I'm great, but if I can't show anyone else how to be great, then how great am I? It's your actions that tell what your faith is. And with your action goes your character because you cannot say that you have great faith and your character doesn't match what you're saying you have faith in. You can't say you believe in God or a higher power, yet you don't rely on or depend on them for anything.

When I say him, God is a spirit. Those who love God must create a spiritual bond in spirit and truth. Your character means everything because it is, in essence, your truth.

So, if your character doesn't align, then that's not your character. Your character and personality traits, along with your faith, work together to bring you to the promise of your dreams, hopes, and desires. How do your actions line up with your words? And how does that display your faith and your character together? Because all of it works together.

When they all align, you'll see more results in your favor. What do your actions speak about your character? What do you say you believe? Do you truly believe, based on your actions, what you say? This is the question I will leave you with regarding the power of your actions over your words.

Faith Without Works Explained

What does faith without works mean? Faith without works is a spiritual analogy, meaning if you're not doing anything to nourish your soul, you won't be able to produce soul-based projects, information, or things that will nourish other people's souls.

You can't just speak and say that that's faith. At some point, your actions must align with what you're saying. If you're saying that you believe, let's say you believe in a new job or a new house, but you're not going out and applying; you're not taking any action that physically demonstrates that you believe what you're saying you believe.

And that's the biggest thing. Like, if you're not able to put some action behind what you're saying, then what you're saying isn't the truth that you believe. Your actions display the truth of what you believe.

So what do you believe? Your faith says I'm healed, but you never go to the doctor. Your faith says I'm healed, but you never do anything to change your diet habits. I'm not saying to cut out everything, but there should be some changes, whether it's increasing water intake, eating smaller meals, or increasing the proportion of vegetables in your diet if your diet allows you to eat a lot of vegetables.

Some people don't know that you can have some health issues that make you not be able to eat vegetables. However, if you have never been in a situation like that or have never known anyone personally who cannot eat vegetables, then you would automatically think that an all-vegetable diet will work for you. However, not all vegetables can be consumed by everyone. Based on somebody else's faith, you go on a diet, but that's not your faith.

You shouldn't base your life on somebody else's faith and think that you're going to get the same result if that's not what God purposed for you in your life. If those are not the goals that he gave you in a vision, then you're working on somebody else's plan, which is not always going to be totally away from your plan or God's promise for your life, but I guarantee it's not going to be the fullness of what God had for you because you're not doing what God showed and told you.

Faith without works is dead; it is lifeless. How can you say you believe if you don't act on that belief?

It's just like saying, You're married, and you want to get pregnant, but you're not having sex. If you are not in a happy place, it can hinder your ability to be intimate with each other in a way that fosters genuine bonding. No Sexual Bonding, No Baby.

When sex becomes a chore, you're not in faith anymore. Marriage is about bonding, loving, coming together, building, growing, and multiplying your seed in the earth. For some, marriage doesn't involve having children, but what are you building within that marriage? What do you see yourself doing long-term, and how do you work towards those goals?

I cannot say that I aspire to win the Nobel Peace Prize, yet I do nothing to serve the community or promote peace.

Taking the time to ensure you are aligned with your purpose can prevent you from taking the wrong path, learning lessons that God didn't intend for you, and having to start back where you left off, relearning what God said. You can work as much as you want, but you're not going to get in by your work alone, especially if you're not doing the work that God assigned for you.

This is bigger than just speaking things into existence. When you speak things into existence, your faith should motivate you to take action to bring them into reality. So, what do you have faith for? How are you going to work to get it? How do you be efficient about getting it done? Think for a second.

It's okay. I want you to know that to demonstrate faith truly, you should create a vision for your life. If you're like me, you probably have two or three vision boards, but you need to see what you're working on in front of you.

If you create a vision board with words or any instructions on it, you should pray and ask God, 'Okay, God, this is the vision you've set for my life.' ' How do I make this vision board a reality in my life? At Speaking Freedom, we're about bringing your dreams to life.

However, to make a dream a reality, you first need to pray about it; you must clarify what the dream is so that you can apply it to your life and bring it to fruition. Once you bring it to pass, you can live in the happy place you dreamed about.

After you pray about it, you must ask God what it will cost you. Ask God what you will have to give up for you to establish the foundation to build on. When you go to build a new house, you visit the office; you ask to see the model, inquire about the available floor plans, and determine what's within your budget.

After you determine what's in your budget, if you put in a contract on an unbuilt home, before you can set up a contract, you have to select the lot. Where is it going to be? How will it sit? Which side is the driveway going to be on? Will there be a garage? Where will the line of my property stop? These are the things that you have to know before you even put your contract in. If you get a contract and haven't seen the property, you could be living on a small piece of land that's not much, and you don't even know.

You have to see what you're getting into, and after the contract, you have to work. You need to gather all your documents and ensure you get approved for the home, as well as obtain the pre-qualification letter. Once you receive the pre-qualification letter, there are still other steps to take to secure the home you plan to put a contract on after selecting the lot. This includes selecting your wall color and floor systems, as well as determining the appearance of the siding or brick.

The first step is learning what's available.

After you learn about the available options, you can ask about your choices and options when buying a home. You still have to wait for the building work to be completed. This is not about buying homes, but it's a great example of what it takes to not only build your faith but also to walk in faith, achieve your dreams, and take your goals from 'I saw' to 'I made it happen' in your life. The work part of your faith matters if you're not willing to do anything, but what you're saying you have faith for, you don't really want it.

If you're not willing to obtain the documents that the builder or finance company requires to approve you for the home and close out the loan, then you're not. Although you write a contract, you're not obligated to the home.

I didn't learn this until after I bought my second home. You're not obligated to that home until the very end until you sign those closing documents. They may say that you can't get your money back. Still, if there is a default on their end, which prevents you from getting approved, and you do not withdraw, you can still get your money back.

That's part of the knowledge you need for your faith.

Within the process of choosing a home, if God tells you, 'Okay, wait a minute, stop; I want you to do something different and pick up and move,' it's because your faith is not strong enough. You won't be able to put in the work to say, ' You know what, hold on, hold that thought; I think I need to make this adjustment. ' See, all of that is work.

Everyone often thinks that work is always about manual labor, but sometimes, work is about your mind's ability to change, adjust, and improve. It is hard to transition from a street thug to corporate America. In general, it's work to figure out, as a single mom, how to be a good mom when the street raised you.

There's nothing that you can say that you have faith for, that you won't have to work for. If you claim to have faith, you must take action to demonstrate it and see the promise fulfilled.

It's like being in a relationship. You say you want a relationship. You must mentally prepare for what you say you want.

You can have faith in forming a meaningful connection, even without leaving the house. You can definitely say you have faith in owning a home, not leave your apartment, and still achieving your dream of homeownership. With most things done online, it's easy to claim faith and acquire certain things without much effort.

But the big things that God has for you are going to supersede just talking about it. You have to move in the direction that your faith and your sole purpose are guiding you. If not, you don't have faith for what you're saying. You have a lot of talk, a lot of wordplay, a lot of hopes, and a lot of dreams. But what are you doing to make it happen for real?

In real life, you don't go from homeless to a mansion from begging on the corner. You transition from being homeless to having a mansion by identifying how you arrived at your current situation, figuring out how to change it to achieve your desired outcome, and then taking the actual steps to get there.

For some, cutting your hair may be a good option, but you also need to be clean and find suitable clothes.

Someone who is underprivileged may need to visit a thrift store, such as Goodwill, to see what they can purchase. They may need to stand on the corner and beg so that they can raise the money to go to Goodwill and buy clothes, which will help them get an interview and secure a job. Places like Love Beyond Walls help homeless people get back on their feet, establish a sense of purpose within themselves, and make them feel human again.

Just because you're homeless doesn't mean you don't have faith. It might mean something placed you in a position where you lost everything. You have to be able to find the ability to be able to trust God to take you from the pit of homelessness to the palace. However, someone has to speak faith into you.

Sometimes, you need a little extra emphasis and extra motivation. The things you can't find within yourself sometimes need to be gained from others. You need to know where to look for inspiration, but you also need to understand your resources to reach your desired destination.

If you're in the music business and trying to secure a record deal, gain notoriety, or achieve some other goal, your first step is to establish your vision. What is your purpose in the vision? What is your end goal? How do you plan to achieve this goal? You're not going to get there sitting twiddling your thumbs. I can guarantee you that.

Even if you're not a musician, if you're trying to get into the business as a manager, an AR, or anything else, you have to work. You cannot claim to have faith in something that you're not willing to work for. The work you need to do might not be a struggle for you because you are gifted in this area, but you will still face challenges.

If you already know what it will take to achieve your goals, then whatever the process is, it won't be a struggle for you because you've already calculated the cost.

Faith without works means that you claim to want something, but you're not willing to do anything to achieve it.

When you say you want something, but you're not willing to do anything to get it, you automatically cancel out the fact that you said you want it, and your faith is dead. That means it's not growing, becoming anything. You can't wallow and think it's going to magically appear if you're not doing anything to get it. You won't get in heaven by your works, but you'll receive your reward for your faith through your works. Your works are the only thing that can bring your dream into action and reveal reality.

What reality are you looking for? Are you looking to maintain your current level of faith, or are you seeking to deepen your spiritual connection? As a new believer, you don't have as many hang-ups as somebody who's been in faith for a while, somebody who's been believing for a while. As a new believer, you don't have as many hiccups or issues with your faith because you haven't experienced it not happening. Most new believers haven't tried to make their own thing because they're solely after God.

Unless they're coming to God as a means of escape from something else or driven by greed, all they know how to do is believe in God. All they know how to do is set their minds high for what's to come.

If God tells a new believer something, nine times out of ten, they will do it without hesitation. This is one of the things that makes the new believer so much more potent than the old believer in some cases because the older believer, once you have tried to put your own thing on what you want God to do and not what God thinks is, then you're more likely not to experience what God has for you. You're more likely not even to get a trickle of what God could do because you're doing your own thing.

God can work in you doing your own thing, but God won't explode your own thing. He won't make your own thing be so big that you can't even fathom what it could be because God's thing is 10 times better than what your own thing is. Unless you're fully aligned with God, you won't see or feel the type of increase and breakthrough that God could bring you.

You must know what you're believing and why you believe it. You have to have the right type of people around you to help you work your faith. You cannot be a person who lives by faith, works by faith, and does everything by faith, and surround yourself with people who are fearful, doubtful, timid, or anything else. People with a negative mindset will not be able to support where you're going because of the defeat they've experienced in their mind, even if they're believers, even if they're your friends, even if they're your mom, dad, uncle, auntie, or sister

Therefore, it is essential to surround yourself with people who can help you understand the importance of nurturing your faith and following God's guidance. The question is, what do you believe in? What are you hoping that God does for you? A more important question: what are you willing to work for? What type of work are you willing to do? See, a portion of your faith, vision, and purpose is about discovering what your purpose is. What are you skilled, talented, and gifted at naturally, not what you have to be forced to do?

There's a significant difference, but these are essential things to know to walk out your faith. It's a faith walk, not a faith sit down, so exercise.

We're talking about turning your literal dreams into reality. The things that people would never believe you could do, you can make happen, but you have to have faith and know how to work your faith. You have to know how to achieve what you say you have faith in. The first key is to put your faith into action, with your words and actions aligning with what you say you believe.

I can share with you my experiences and insights about faith, and tell you about the many ways God has blessed me. However, if you are not willing to do what God is telling you to do, then it won't benefit you. God can do the same things or something different for you because not everyone believes the same. Everybody doesn't expect the same. Not everyone wants the same things.

My role here is to help you grow in your faith and become strong in it so you can discover your purpose, live it out, and ultimately receive the promises of God in your real life, not just discuss them. The goal here is to transition you from discussing faith to living in faith, ultimately to having a faith-based life. It's not just about talking faith.

No faking it until you make it. We are after real results. Anybody can say they trust God. Do you have results? Show me where you trusted God, and it worked. Show me where you walked out your faith and applied the work to what you said you believed, and you did what God told you to do, then received the outcome, and the outcome was magnificent.

Show me that, and I'll show you how your faith got you there. I'll show you what steps you took, what things you need to redo, and what things you need to apply to the next faith move that can keep you having a faithful life and on track to reaching every last desire that you have and obtaining some things that you didn't even know were possible.

Chapter 3: How God Speaks (Overview)

Before you can discern what God is saying, you must understand how God speaks. This may seem out of place, as we're emphasizing the importance of walking in faith, learning your faith, and making it a living reality.

To live Faith, for your actions to be more powerful and your words to be more effective, and to do better and achieve greater things, you must be able to hear God's voice. Do you know how God sounds? How does God speak to you? The voice in your head, what does it sound like? Is it negative or positive? We're going to explore how God speaks and learn how to listen to God. This is one of the most vital things you will ever learn.

So, what does God sound like? Let's start by acknowledging that God is both very real and positive. God will speak things that you couldn't imagine but that you can feel, and you know that it's obtainable if you put in the work. Here are some types of things that God says: "It's possible; only believe, no doubt, no fear."

Although I'm not a fan of religion, to learn how God speaks, I recommend the Bible. The only reason I recommend the Bible or other spiritual books is that they contain stories in chapters and books that record who said what, when they said it, and how they acted upon what they heard from God.

To get to the who, what, when and, where, and how God speaks, you have to get a general idea of what God will say, how God moves, what God does when he does.

It's simple, but it's complicated because many things can sound like God, but that doesn't mean they are God. To learn how God speaks.

I suggest reading spiritual books by other spiritually inclined individuals who have had a profound experience of God. Consider books about individuals who are psychic mediums, specifically spiritualists who have felt God's presence in their lives, who get goosebumps when speaking about God, and who can convey messages that they believe God has communicated. You can know it's from God when you haven't shared it with anyone else. This is how God speaks.

If you have any spiritual gifts, research them to learn more about your purpose. Speakingfreedom.org has several personality, spiritual gifts, and purpose-based quizzes to help you further your journey with God.

God probably will not be in your head, saying, "Yes, my child, this is what I want from you," but I can say that God will send you a sign. God will also send someone to inform you of what He said, and He'll give you multiple signs; it's up to you to act on them.

God speaks in many ways. God could be speaking to you through this book. God could speak to you through each lesson I give, through each lecture, book, talking point, and every aspect of what I do. God could speak through all of these. I can't tell you what will resonate in your soul from God.

Your personal relationship with God has to be a one-on-one relationship. God should be closer than your best friend. If you're married, your spouse should be your best friend; however, the relationship you have with God should be deeper than the one you have with your spouse. When you deepen your relationship with God, you'll likewise deepen your relationship with your spouse.

A deepened relationship with God is not about attending church or being religious. You must take it a step further and commune with God, engaging in real-life conversations with your Creator. Saying things like: "Hey God, I just wanted to let you know I love you today. Man, could you understand or believe that that just happened right there?

Personally, I converse with God as if I believe God speaks to me. I believe God says some weird things sometimes. Many people do not believe in cussing in the same sentence, mentioning God. I never cuss at God, but in conversation, I express myself to God the way that I am. You could fake with God, but God knows your heart.

In your mind, if you're thinking a cuss word, guess what? God knows in your mind you're thinking a cuss word. You could say darn. If you're thinking damn and you say darn, you should have just said damn.

The point is when speaking with God, for God to be real with you, you have to be real with God. You cannot put on a facade when you're going to God. God sees all things.

Before you were placed on this planet, he knew who you were. What's the point of going to God with old rhetoric if you're not even going to walk out your faith to begin with? Because nine times out of 10, if God told you and spoke to you and "thus saith, this is what you need to doeth." Eventually, you're likely to get lost.

You'll be left thinking, "God, what are you saying? What do you want me to do? I don't understand. Please help me get it." However, if you approach God directly, you will receive a direct answer.

God knows, just like you go to your physical dad and tell them everything that's going on. They usually know when something is going on with their child.

When you understand what's going on with your child, you listen and offer recommendations. God works the same way.

Ask for a sign.

Be specific when you pray to God so God can be specific in his answers. How you pray to God, being specific with God, and knowing what you want can be a little bit more important than actually hearing from God or knowing how to hear from God.

If you're not praying the right thing, you're not going to want to hear what God is telling you anyway. Let's be honest here. If you're praying for a Benz, but God is saying to start with this Hyundai, you're likely to reject God because you're thinking, 'God, I said I wanted the Benz.'

God might be telling you, 'I need you to be faithful over this Hyundai so that I can give you a Benz with favor.' Oftentimes, people think that God makes things fall out of the sky, but he doesn't.

This isn't "a cloudy chance of meatballs" or something. How God works is that you pray, ask, and put in the work by following His directions.

Okay, God has to use a resource to get it to you. He may allow somebody else to supplement with a resource. God is not a physical person. He, much like what we read about Jesus, makes Himself present within the person, place, or thing He chooses to use to reach you with what you're asking for.

Some want to hear from God, and he'll speak to them clearly. It may be in a dream, a vision, or maybe someone who comes up to you and says, 'Something just told me to tell you that you're amazing, that you're going to achieve all your hopes, all your dreams, all your desires, but you have to apply what you know inside."

In that case, if you don't think you know enough, take the time to learn more about it. Remember, the only way you're going to get to what God has for you is by doing more, applying more, having more ambition, and more time with God set aside away from everything so God can speak to you and so that you can learn how to speak to God properly.

Properly speaking to God is simply having a conversation, being able to be real with God, and not having to approach God with a facade. If you approach God with a facade, you're not being honest with God. What can you obtain if you're lying to God or trying to deceive God? God (The Universe) is the fullness of everything that you are and knows everything that you will be.

What are you willing to do? What are you willing to ask God for? Whatever you're willing to ask God for will sometimes reveal what you're willing to hear from God.

God may be speaking to you right now, but depending on what you've asked, you may not be willing or ready to listen to what God is saying. God is not going to tell you anything negative, only the truth in Love.

God may sing you through a negative time. God may allow a path to open up for you that seems like it will tear you apart. But this is where hearing from God is the most important because on that path, even though it seems like it's going to tear you apart, that's the path that God created for you to become great.

If you're a believer in Jesus, do you think that Jesus would have been able to endure the cross without first being tested those 40 days? God wouldn't allow the test unless the test were in preparation for something greater. That's how you have to look at life.

You must be able to tune out everything else and truly focus on God. For some, that will be hard, odd, and strange, but you do. Nobody can confirm what God is telling you if you've never heard from God yourself. I can speak into your life, but if you've never heard something from God yourself, you will doubt, and you might not understand.

Anything that I say should be confirmation. If not, then you're more likely to be pulled and tugged into many things that God may not have for you. Random people can say, 'God said this' or 'God said that. ' If you get enough people telling you what God said without you hearing from God for yourself or without it being confirmation, then you'll be scatterbrained, tossed around wondering how you got to where you find yourself.

You'll be going everywhere. You'll be trying to do everything. You're trying to be, you know what I'm saying, what everybody else wants you to be.

And you haven't even had the time to sit down with God. And then that's how people get into places where they don't belong, or they feel like they're being tested. And then, sometimes, you can hear from God, and God will tell you, ' Go ahead.'

It might be hard. You might not get the result that you think you're supposed to get from doing this, but the result that I have for you is better. So keep going.

Oh, I know this seems like a tough thing. I know it seems peculiar. I know people will judge you for this.

I know, I know, I know. Its purpose is to guide you to the things you desire. , what do you do to get there? Do you listen to God? Do you listen to your elders? Do you listen to yourself or what? What are you going to do? How does God speak to you? In what ways are you asking God to speak is a great question.

Are you asking God to show you a sign, to speak to you in dreams, to send someone your way to help you confirm what he told you today?

These are essential to having faith. Some people know how to hear from God, but do they hear what they want from God or do what God says? You can want to hear one thing, and God says something else. If you keep doing what you want God to say instead of what God said, you're not likely to get the results you prayed for.

Focus on getting results, exercising your faith, and becoming great.

What's great? Greatness is being better than you were before. Greatness is doing things in a way you've never done before, starting a new path, setting trends, and being an influence amongst your peers.

Will you be great? Will you listen to God? When you learn how to listen to God, are you willing to share with others how to hear, pray to, believe in, and experience God, living their truth, and experiencing the reality that started out as a dream?

If you're thinking we haven't covered "How to Hear from God," from what I've said since I started this Chapter, then you're not paying attention.

Learning to hear from God is about establishing a mental process that aligns with the universe, allowing for a one-on-one meditation with the universe. Hearing from God is a personal experience.

People hear God differently and at different times. Not everybody sees or dreams the same.

So it's about what makes it an experience for you. What did you ask God for? How did you ask God to show up? How did you ask God to confirm what he said he would do?

You have to ask God for confirmation and what plans God has for your life.

You have to speak to God to be open to hearing from God. How do you plan to hear from God if you don't have any time set aside just for God?

Are you willing to say to God, "I just want to live the life that you created me to live." and then watch God begin to unfold it before your eyes?

Create your vision board.

You can start small; I recommend it. When you create a vision board, the Law of Attraction takes effect, and you "speak things into existence" by putting your intentions out there. Immediately, you start seeing things begin to change. Even the bible tells you to "write the vision and make it plain so that others can run with it that read/ see it."

Your life changes, and your vision begins to take root within the soil that you've been placed over, allowing your roots to grow strong and continue to flourish over time. You must be willing to listen only to God and not let anyone else distract you. Focus solely on God and what God wants for you.

Find people who show real results.

It's not always your pastor or spiritual leader. Sometimes, it may be someone that God brings into your life so that you can see how God works.

That doesn't mean the person will be in your life forever. What it means is that you must be open to what God wants to do with you and how He wants to do it. Be open and ready for change and adjust accordingly.

The spiritual life is not an easy one. People think that when you start believing in God, trusting God, and hearing from God, then life becomes boring. But this is the most exciting ride of your life because you never know exactly what God is going to do with you to affect others and build you stronger.

God will give you a blueprint. He will give you the plan and the vision, but not every detail is always available. If you knew that you had to go through a struggle, lose that person, and other challenges, some people would back out. Some people wouldn't even go forward becoming stuck in their faith. Those are the people who typically become elders or mature believers. You have to find someone with real-time results.

Don't follow anybody or be around anyone who can barely believe for something small. They believe in/for God to talk to them, but you believe in/for God to show you Him. Speaking to God and seeing God are two totally different things.

The blessing is not the result, it's the result of the blessing. The blessing is the ability to learn, trust, hear, and be one with God to carry out and see what God is telling you to do.

The result of the blessing is whatever the manifestation is. Whatever you receive on the end, on the back end. If you're in music or in a place where you receive a front-end deposit and a back-end payment once services are complete, plus any extras.

Your faith is the deposit, front-end. Your work is what gets you the results, in the back end. You can't get the back end if you don't put in the work. Even though you have the contract, the faith, and the vision, you still need to put in the effort. If you don't put in the work, that back end doesn't come.

You can have your faith, dreams, beliefs, and religion. If you don't put in your work, talk, knowledge, and actions with God, you won't bring your dreams into reality.

This is not about being negative. This is about being realistic. Do you want real results, or do you want to play? Do you want to make mud pies or create glamorous cakes? You decide. I can't decide that for you.

What I can do is help you learn to recognize God. You may see God in the animals that come around. Personally, I believe I see God in the weather and in creatures of the earth. I see God in every single thing that goes on around me. I could be praying something, going through something, and guess what? He'll send an animal.

I'll look up what that animal means, and it'll reveal something that will provide and secure my faith, comfort whatever I'm experiencing at that moment, and serve as a confirmation. Most people miss God's confirmations and God speaking because they're waiting for someone to come out of the sky and say, " Hey, you, this is what I need from you. ' This is what I have for you. Do this."

When God may send someone that suggests something very small, but you have to be open to hearing that. He may send the animal, which means your blessings are in your next steps, but you have to be able to hear that.

You have to be able to see and k to, hmm, what does that deer mean? Hmm, what do those packs of pigs mean? What does the flock of geese mean? What does a snake mean? You have to learn more than what you've been taught. You have to learn the history of where you come from. It's so many things that come and help you build faith so that you're not a religious nut but that you're a spiritual fruit.

This is the thing. To hear from God, you must learn yourself.

Chapter 4: Self-Knowledge is God Knowledge

Let's start here. You're made in God's image. Before God sent you to this earth, he knew who you were already.

Before you were even formed or thought of in your mother's mind or belly, God knew who you were, knew who he wanted you to be, knew what you would do, knew what you were capable of, and knew what would be your shortcomings. So if those things are true based on general knowledge, based on what we know to believe, what we think, the way we feel on the inside, what we've studied and learned through history, as well as the Bible. The Bible is widely regarded as the most well-known spiritual book in the world, and it has a profound influence on our culture today, which is why I am discussing it.

So if all of those things are true about you and about what God knew about you, then take this thought for a second. There is nothing that you can do that God didn't know that you would do before your birth date. Even if you think back to Eve, God knew that she would bite the apple beforehand.

I don't even want to say 'apple'. God knew that she would bite the fruit beforehand, but He wanted to see her response —the result of her doing her own thing

If God made you in his image, that means that every single thing about you from birth is in alignment with God. Whether you understand every single thing about you or every single thing about God, those two things are dependent upon you. Knowing yourself is parallel to knowing God because you're made in God's image.

The more you know about yourself, the more you have an understanding of why God made you and what you're created here to do. And in knowing yourself, you learn more about God because you're made in His image.

Every light, every dislike, every thought, everything is crafted after God. Here's the tricky part: whether you choose to focus on the negative or the positive is up to you. God doesn't want you to look at the negative, I'm quite sure.

Will you be able to see the positive side of things based on your life experience? Can you reflect on your life experiences and see how God was using them to bring you to where you are today? Or where your dreams can take you tomorrow? Self-knowledge, being a form of God knowledge, means that the more acquainted you are with your good qualities, the more you're acquainted with your greatness.

Conversely, the more acquainted you are with your shortcomings, the more you'll be acquainted with yourself. This can work to make you better as you ultimately come to understand God's purpose for your life. God knew that you would have shortcomings. He knew that greatness would be within you.

If God knows all things from the number of hairs on your head, then why wouldn't he understand who you are? Why wouldn't he want you to know every single good, bad, or indifferent thing? Most things that you feel are bad about you aren't necessarily bad, they are things that someone told you, and you look at yourself as though that thing is wrong with you. Basing your life on what somebody else told you rather than on what God is trying to show you or has already shown you will lead to self-doubt and confusion within.

It's about learning God better by knowing yourself better. Saying to God… "Okay, God, why did you make me like this? I need to know why I am this way. Why do I have this big mouth? Why am I shy? Why do I have this way about me? Why do I look like this? Why are my hips shaped like this? Why does my mind think like this? Why do I like this this way and that that way? Why?"

The more you know why something or what changed your view about something, the more you can go to God and say, okay, God, how does this grow me into my future, my purpose, my life purpose, my soul purpose, and what you say should be the desire of my heart because I only want what you want. If you're reading this book right now, you want what God wants for your life, and you're trying to figure out how to get there.

Speaking Freedom will help you obtain what it is you're looking for from God. However, you must recognize his voice and have faith.

You have to know yourself so you can understand not only why God put you on this planet, on this earth, on this ground right in this time, but how to be a better you so that you can accomplish whatever those dreams are, those things that leave you up at night that makes you want to keep going. How do you accomplish those things if you don't know who you are? If you don't know your likes and your dislikes? If you don't know why you have this habit versus that habit or why you choose this way over that way?

That means going back and learning about yourself, figuring out, ' Okay, when did I become afraid of this? When did I begin to view this this way? Why don't I like this particular thing? What have I grown up around that changed or developed my view? The better you know yourself, the better that you will know God because you will be able to figure out your why?'

Learn. The more you learn about yourself, the more you learn about your dreams and why your vision is so this way why your vision is clear or why you are unable to tap into your purpose. When you desire to live on purpose, for purpose, because of purpose, and you want to please God and not just look good for people, when you desire something more out of life, you have to teach yourself so you can know why you desire more.

Learn what you do naturally with No help, no sedatives, no supplements. By yourself what comes naturally to you to do, help, or be within the world? What's natural? What flows? Some people are great chefs. Some people are great caretakers. Some people were born to be doctors.

Personally, here at Speaking Freedom, our life culture was born to help people heal, to help them become whole in mind, heart, and soul. That's what we were created for. Anyone who joins our team or is already a member is expected to help others grow.

We believe and will do it with our whole hearts without any extra effort. We are here to help you figure out who you are. Why do you like that? Why do you walk that way? Why do you talk that way? How do your family and upbringing help shape you into who you were called to be on earth? These are the important things.

These are the things that help connect you not only with God but also help you understand your purpose. To know God is to know your purpose, to live, and to walk it out faithfully. However, you must have faith in yourself and God.

But to believe in yourself, you have to accept all the good, all the bad, all the indifferent, everything that ever has been criticized. You have to learn to embrace yourself in every way, shape, form, or fashion. It's not just how you think.

You have to embrace how you look. You must understand that if you change something about yourself that God didn't instruct you to change, you may be disrupting something else, not just for yourself but also for someone else. God may have had something in mind to meet you somewhere, with someone, at some place.

The moment you change something about who God created you to be, you disrupt the atmosphere. You toss up everything. A shift occurs when you make unauthorized changes without understanding why God created you in a certain way. In such cases, you will try to change who you are to fit in.

When you change yourself, you miss some of God's blessings because you no longer appear to be the person God created you to be, having changed into something else. You're not you anymore. You're not whoever it is that God created this purpose for, this person for, this place for, to meet you here in this certain particular manner.

you've thrown it all off because you didn't understand yourself. You didn't love yourself because you couldn't love yourself completely until you understood every nook and cranny about yourself. That's why you seek out your own soul salvation because you have to teach yourself to bring out the best in yourself, your children, your family, or anyone that surrounds you.

If you don't know yourself, then you'll always be subject to what other people think, what they're going through, or what they say. The only thing that we desire you to be subject to is God. Again, we are not religious.

If you are religious, then we thank God for you and your growing patterns. We thank God that you are here with us, seeking to absorb new information so you can grow in new ways. Don't stop whatever is helping you grow, learn, and draw closer to God Himself, rather than merely becoming comfortable with the traditions of someone else's experience with God.

Your desire to have your own journey, your own experiences with God, is a testament to your design. You're meant to have your own legacy to pass down to your children, who will then pass it down to their children so they can understand the path, plan, and role they play in their lineage on this earth. What's purposeful for them? Some of it's connected to history, and history is what shapes the culture, which we'll cover in a moment.

Chapter 5: The Lessons of No Results

Your results are like the fine, intricate line on which you measure everything. All of your successes, failures, and everything you do can be measured by the results you achieve. It's essential to look at your results to see the outcome and how you arrived at that point. Review how you got to that particular spot and What you could have done to alter the outcome. The results are your measuring tape.

When reviewing things, it's essential to recognize that if you're not satisfied with the result, you can make adjustments. Based on your outcome, determine what needs to be changed, what should remain unchanged, and what may require only slight adjustments.

When you're reviewing your results, you have to ask, 'Okay, how did I achieve this?' ' What decisions did I make that made the result this instead of that? If it's a desired result, then you know what you need to continue doing to ensure that you achieve the desired outcome. If the result you desire changes throughout the process of achieving it, then how can you adjust to reach the next goal, the next result, the next thing?

When you get results that you didn't want, the ones that were unexpected and a little off, those are just as important because, in those results, you can go back and ask, ' How did I make this mistake? '

Let's say you go to school. You decide that you want to take a particular class or that your major is going to be medicine. You're going to pursue general studies so that you can get into your major

You decide that you want to become a nurse, but then you realize that somewhere in there, the results you desire and the results you're aiming for aren't even the same thing. If you start pursuing a career as a nurse and aren't doing well, you may need to reconsider it. What can you do differently? Do you genuinely enjoy this subject, or is it just something I'm doing because I know it pays well?

If your results are all contingent upon making money or the profit that you can get from it, then your results will be limited to what money can buy, what money can get you, or where money can take you.

When you go beyond results being solely based on money, you realize that reward and results are two different things. A reward is what you receive for doing something. In most cases, when a reward is given for an act, it is something we appreciate, and we would like to present you with one. Those two things, unless you're doing something to get awarded or to be rewarded, don't necessarily mean that that's the result.

You should have different levels and layers to your results; your results should not be based solely on material things or spiritual things. Your results have to be well-rounded.

But that depends on where your thinking is. How are you thinking? What are you thinking? What is it that you desire to have? What is it that you're trying to get? Where do you see yourself going? See, your results are not necessarily only when you get them. Results are like goals.

What goals do you have? What results do you desire? Where do you see yourself being? Where would you like to be? Where could you be? Give me all of those things. Please share everything you know about yourself and then describe where you envision yourself going.

If you're going to have faith in something, you must set a goal for your faith to achieve. You can have faith simply for being alive.

If you're in this book, it means you're seeking something more out of life. And you would like for us to help you get there. You would like us to help you understand how to think more effectively, be more effective, and live a better life.

It's based on where you want your results. What goals do you have? Because those are the results that you're setting yourself up to receive. And then you take these steps and figure out, ' Okay, this is how I get here. ' This is how I got here.

This is how I got the results. You realize that this is how you get the results, and you learn from it; okay, what do I need to redo? What do I need to take away? What do I need to stop? As your results improve, your goals also increase, allowing your results to continue growing and ultimately enabling you to accomplish more. Then you're able to say, ' Okay, I'm accomplishing something. '

Faith is important for new believers. You've to set goals because if not, you'll be just circling around, and you won't even know if you've reached the place you need to be. Most new believers are fresh.

They have new ideals, and they're the ones trying to help grow a place while also growing themselves in general. When you encounter older believers or the elders, if they've been discouraged, then they can be discouraging. They can hinder others' goal setting, results, or flourishing in a way that, in the mind of a new believer, they should not.

New believers often come to realize that people become stagnant when they don't get any results or achieve results but don't know what they did to obtain them. It's not only important to get the results, but it's also very important to know how you get the results because the result is pointless if you do not know how to achieve that result again, aside from the temporary gratification.

You have to know how to get that particular thing again, and when you're a new believer, you're able to keep doing and keep doing.

You're able to focus, so you don't have to be tainted with all the doubt and misbelief that comes with unrealistic goals or unattainable results. This highlights the importance of maintaining a new believer's mindset. It's essential that just because you grow older in the church, it doesn't mean you forget to renew your mind daily.

Renewing your mind means gaining a fresh understanding daily, learning something new every day, and taking better care of yourself daily. When you are a new believer, maintaining a fresh and untainted state allows you to grow and soar, becoming the best you can be. Once you learn who you are, what you want out of life, and the things you desire, you're able to tackle your goals, which will be connected to your purpose.

Once you learn the formula for results, you can keep getting more results. You continue to grow from making the same faith move. You may make adjustments here and there. You may do something different to make sure that you're getting the different things that you desire out of life, but in totality, you're making the same moves over and over again.

People who fail tend to repeat the same mistakes, thinking they'll get different results with the same approach. When you start succeeding, rinse and repeat.

When you find your rhythm to success, you don't stop following it. Don't allow anyone to get in the way of that rhythm. You keep going.

Keep going. As you continue to move forward, you establish faith-based results based on the changes you make from the results you didn't achieve. Then, you can learn, grow, and help someone else because you can't help anyone else until you're succeeding in the way you desire to succeed, achieving the results you desire. That is the key factor in growing up having child-like faith every day.

It takes a mature person to have a faith that's like a child's, yet still be mature, handle responsibilities, and do all the things necessary to help the community. It takes a childlike faith to accomplish many things. That means believing what you can't see, yet knowing it's there and achieving it.

There's nothing wrong with being a mature believer, but ensure that the results you desire are being achieved. Once you start obtaining these results, take note of how you're achieving them. No matter where you're, take note of how you're achieving the result, whether good or bad. For the poor result, the notes are provided to help you understand how to improve it. For a good result, continue to succeed and maintain it so you know how to sustain it.

The whole goal is success. The ultimate goal is to live out your purpose. That's success.

Happiness is success.

Perceived happiness and success are not always accumulated by money, but if you want it, you have to put forth the effort into it. You have to be willing to do what other people aren't willing to do.

Set goals that yield results and know how to balance your outcomes. What did you want to receive, and what did you get? Did you get what you expected? Did you get more, less, or something entirely different? Those are important things to take note of, and once you do, you can learn, grow, and improve. Then, you can advance, study, and do more.

The goal is the longevity of faith, obtaining the promise of your purpose, achieving a whole and total life of excellence, peace, and a sound mind and good judgment while strengthening the community around us as we strengthen ourselves. That's the goal, and goals start with small, achievable results.

Chapter 6: Small Results, Big Effects

You don't need to be in your first year or aspire to be like someone who's been doing it for 30 years. No. Every small success you achieve significantly strengthens your faith.

I don't care if someone is giving you something you didn't expect. No matter the outcome, you must begin. Your confidence builders are the small things, the unexpected moments, and those aspects that others often overlook, yet you recognize the joy and light in them.

Observe the sky. Observe the moon. Observe the stars.

Observe the clouds. Notice the plants. Acknowledge all the things surrounding you.

Enjoy and embrace the process, then measure your success and build your confidence with small victories. You landed a new job. That's a victory.

You got a new house, Victory. You've got an apartment, a new car, a new degree, and you're back in school. Those are all victories. These are confidence builders that you'll have along the way as long as you continue to work at your goals. Where you start is how your confidence is built. Just start somewhere.

The sooner you start, the better you'll be because your confidence grows with time in that craft or in your faith for whatever it is you are pursuing.

Your confidence doesn't stem from anything other than being happy with the results. The goals that you set for yourself and the results that you've obtained are based on what you're doing, how you're moving, how you're believing, how you see yourself, and how you know yourself. If you know yourself better, you can base your decisions on what will make you happy rather than what everyone else is doing. Many people do what everybody else is doing when they go home; they're not happy.

The goal is to get to know yourself so you can understand what makes you happy. If you know what brings you joy, it'll help you avoid mistakes. It'll help you avoid some of the pitfalls and build up your confidence along the way.

If you don't get the job you thought you wanted, perhaps God has something better in mind, so keep going. Don't let that deter or disturb you on your journey and what God has in store for you in the long run. As you move forward, little by little, with each small victory and each result, you continue to build. You'll come to realize that all those little things were actually the big things because they've brought you to a new place.

It can take time to realize that you're somewhere new and all those little things that happened pushed you into your destiny. You have to open your mind to that and be ready to receive that.

Achieving those small victories helps you grow. Then, when the time comes, you realize that you are in a different place, and God has positioned you there. That's when you know your faith is working and understand how to apply it continually. Those small victories are what you note to achieve your main result.

Be reminded that passion leads to purpose. The reason I am here is that I became passionate about learning myself, and the more I learned, the more I understood my purpose in life.

The more purposeful I have become in life, the clearer my path to purpose has become, rather than pursuing things. It might sound strange because most people aren't accustomed to being passionate about non-sexual matters. Being passionate about life allows you to recognize and pursue opportunities you might not have otherwise considered.

The more passion you invest, even in the face of setbacks or mistakes, the more you learn to pick yourself up, dust yourself off, and head in a new direction.

If you recall, when you're thinking about the results, once you start achieving those results, it will transform your passion into purpose. I'm talking about how it will elevate you so much that you won't have a choice but to recognize when you're in your purpose.

You'll be able to feel it in your bones when you're purposeful. You'll know it before anyone else knows it because you'll become more passionate about it, and you'll do it effortlessly. Being able to do things effortlessly is because you're doing it with purpose and passion. When you're passionate about something, you're purposeful about doing it.

When you're passionate about something, you'll do things intentionally and with purpose. You're going to ensure this is done the right way and that everything comes together. Harness your passion to achieve your desired results and ultimately fulfill your purpose. How do your passion and your results connect you to your purpose? If you're passionate about achieving results, whether good or bad, they will be purposeful.

Your results will help guide you in where to put your passion. Your results will help you discern what is purposeful in life and what is not. The more passionate you are about achieving results, the more purposeful you become. As a result, you'll be able to apply your faith and see that it's bearing fruit. You will be able to know and hope and grow with

God in a way that you've never imagined before.

This is for everyone. Everyone can benefit from growth in their faith and learning more. Fresh insights on how to approach spiritual, physical, emotional, and financial matters can help everyone grow. These are the areas we cater to, guiding you to understand how you got here, what steps you took, and how to recreate success consistently and intentionally.

The more you act with purpose, the more passionate you'll be about your work. As you start to see results, your passion intensifies. Achieving your goals will elevate your passion because you'll be able to envision, attain, and feel the success you're experiencing rather than just anticipating it in the future.

Those small results are victories; each level you reach and each layer you unveil is purposeful. As you engage more with your purpose, you'll align better with it, leading to increased passion and success in every area of your life. That's life enhancement- what we're here for. Do you see how everything aligns?

Your passion can lead to your purpose because you have faith, even when you can't see the results. This faith strengthens your passion, refines your purpose, and enables you to achieve the results you desire.

The questions I'm asking are so that you know what to ask yourself later. Not just to be asking but so that you know how to measure within yourself.

What are you doing to get the result? What result are you getting? Is this the result that you desire, or do you desire something different? Is this your faith? Are you fresh-minded like a child towards what you're saying that you believe? Do you trust God with all of your heart, mind, and understanding? If a person is an atheist, do they trust themselves with all their heart, mind, and understanding to get you to whatever it is you were placed on Earth to achieve? Remember, even if a person is an atheist, they were placed on Earth for something and should be trying to identify that.

It's all about love. It's not about religion.

It's not about what anybody thinks.

It's about being in love, showing love, walking in love, and receiving love. That's what God.

It's about helping you grow into your soul's purpose. Religion often clouds many minds because they lack knowledge of history and where they come from, which prevents them from experiencing the fullness of God. This is true whether you believe in Muhammad, Buddha, or Jesus, are an atheist, or hold any other belief. I'm not here to judge you.

I'm here to love you, help you see clearly, and support you in living well, being good, and treating those around you well, without expecting anything in return. If you're doing it for that, then you know you've already achieved your result. If you want to grow and receive all that God has for you. If you want to grow in the fullness of your purpose being placed on this planet, then you have to let some stuff go.

You have to grow, and you have to look within to see that's where your history comes in.

Chapter 7: Learn History (Knowledge of Self & The World)

When discussing history, we can delve deeply into it or approach it from a surface level.

When determining what you like and dislike, it ultimately comes down to self-awareness and understanding yourself. Your environment can shape those things as well as who you were raised around. These factors can also be shaped by where you were raised.

Many different factors can shape those things. If you know your history, if you understand where your grandmother came from, where your mother came from, and the type of environment they grew up in, then it'll help you understand why you were either raised or treated the way you were. However, understanding how they grew up, what they had to deal with, and what their injustices were will help you understand your own.

It helps you understand who you are as a person, as there are often things like mindsets, strengths, and weaknesses that are similar. Different people have various blood types. Based on their blood type, they may require different kinds of food to support the growth, learning, and development of their strengths. Certain temperaments exist, and families of people tend to have particular tendencies.

When considering your family history, think about where your grandmother was born. Do you have any Native American ancestry in your family? Do you know anything about the other Americas? Do you know anything about the history of your country, of your land, of your city? Do you know the history of your family?

It's the smallest thing that you should want to know. Where did your religion come from? Where did the pyramids come from? I can't answer where the pyramids came from, but you get the point.

Don't take anything at face value, not yourself or the people around you. The only things you need to take at a surface level are things that you're not interested in.

You don't have to dig deep into everything. Whatever your calling, your interest will follow. Whatever your purpose is, where your tendencies will lead.

The more you learn about your history, your family history, and the people around you, the more you understand their background because one of the people who surround you may fall into a different path or start doing something different. You need to know how to help your friends.

You need to know how to help you because this isn't about anybody else. Of course, when you're strong and knowledgeable, you're able to accomplish more if you start by helping yourself. Once you're strong, you'll be able to help everyone around you.

You can start within your immediate circle, and even if they say no, you've offered to help everyone. However, you can't help people if you don't know how to assist them, and I'm not talking about prying or being nosy.

How do you help them grow? As a life coach here at Speaking Freedom, we have extraordinary ways to help people grow. We identify with who they are, and then we help them grow from where they are into who they aspire to be. We try not to pry into people's personal lives unless they allow us into their personal lives. Still, we instruct them on how to use their history to identify areas where they can make adjustments to break generational curses. Guiding them into new generational surpluses, making life better, and changing so they can know where they came from and where they're going.

It all goes back to your results and where you want to be in life. Are you reaching a new goal? Are you doing something different, or are you on the same track? If you don't even know, then you can't be inspired. Personally, I didn't know all that my grandmother had done in the community. I'm interested in that it makes sense; it aligns more with my life and purpose, and I'm able to embrace what I'm called to do in life more because I know where I came from, sacrifices that she had to make, the things she did to help her flourish, and results she got. I learned that I could do something different than what I thought was available because I didn't know any more than what was in front of me.

I only saw the surface level, but when you have surface-level things, you don't know that it's something deeper than that. It helps you to embrace where you're supposed to be going in your calling and what God has in store for you. If you know that your ancestors achieved certain milestones, then you realize that you can follow in their footsteps.

It's about discovering your why and personal motivation. You were born here into a family with a particular bloodline. No matter how it varies or strays, there are some similarities that stem from that lineage and core aspects that you will find in your personality, mannerisms, or thinking; there are things that are inherent.

If you're with your family, it will make a difference in who you are, how you are, and how you move.

Just because you're in the same family doesn't mean you'll all be exactly alike. That doesn't mean everyone will be happy about your success. If you know where you come from, then you can better understand how to move forward.

Every part of you is special and needed, and everything you've been through is necessary.

Everything that you're going to endure is going to be worth it. You need a foundation, and that starts with where you come from.

To know where you come from, you must first figure out who you are at your core. When you know where you come from, you can understand things about yourself. Once you know your ancestors, you can gain a deeper understanding of your family's history.

When you know more about yourself, you can understand why you move forward purposefully, with meaning, logic, and skill, while managing your emotions with little emotional attachment. These are the things we're here to help you supplement for growth. We don't want you to become dependent on speaking freedom.

We aim to cultivate interdependence, enabling us all to thrive together in our world, culture, and society. I want to leave you with some final thoughts. Whenever you venture to achieve something great, explore the new, or pursue the different, anticipate that some people may not be pleased, especially those who lack the skills to do it themselves, struggle to succeed, or require considerable assistance.

My advice to you is to Never give up, never quit, and never allow other people to discourage you, even just a little bit. Be great on purpose.

Speaking Freedom Books   The Unknow Power

Thank you for purchasing this book from Speaking Freedom. Please listen to the end for further enjoyment. Only God can be perfect, and everybody makes mistakes, so don't be hard on yourself.

Have a good day. This has been The Unknown Power. Please check out our Instagram page, Speaking Freedom.

Thank you for your purchase. Please check out our
other books.

Spiritual Human Behavior
Faith 101
Faith 201
Faith 301
Faith 401
It's My Time

Speaking Freedom Books   The Unknow Power

After Thoughts & Words from Xavier & Nya Myers

From 7 yr old Nya Myers & 8yr old Xavier Myers

When this book was recorded as a audiobook my children added commentary at the end of the book. To maintain the integrity of the original book.
I have included their contributions!

Speaking Freedom is the reason I'm still speaking freedom!

This is Speaking Freedom and we love the world and I mean she's my mirror she's the greatest in the whole world Speaking Freedom like enhancements here and we'll fix you up What do you do for the world? I need you to face the mic and I need you to say it right.

Nya: My mommy is my hero she's the greatest in the whole world My mommy is my hero she's the greatest in the whole world My mommy is my hero she's the greatest in the whole world My mommy is my hero she's the greatest in the whole world Go.

Xavier: This is Speaking Freedom and we love to love.

Thank you for your purchase and for listening we hope your life's enhanced. Lovin' for a lifestyle

Xavier: You said Lovin' for a livin' is a lifestyle Lovin' is a livin' for a lifestyle

Nya & Xavier: Lovin' is a
Kaci: Not so loud

Nya & Xavier: Lovin' is a livin' for a lifestyle Lovin' for a livin' is a lifestyle

Kaci: Thank you

Xavier: We messed it up because of Nya, She made me mess "What do you do for the world?"

Nya & Xavier: Lovin' is a livin' for a lifestyle!

Kaci: Nya Y'all too loud

Xavier: That was Nya's doing

Kaci: Y'all too loud

Xaiver: That was Naya's doing

Xavier & Nya: "Lovin' for a livin' is a lifestyle" Lovin' is a livin' for a lifestyle Lovin' for a livin' is a lifestyle Lovin' is a livin' for a lifestyle

Kaci: Keep singin'

Nya & Xavier: Lovin' for a livin' is a lifestyle

Kaci: Come back over here we recordin' this... Don't do it so loud

Nya & Xavier: for a lifestyle

Xavier: How long is this going to take?

Kaci: until it's over

Nya: Lovin' for a livin' is a lifestyle... It's gonna take forever?

Xaiver: We need to hurry up because we're wasting time

Loving for a Living Explained:

So we need to tell everyone what this is about Lovin' for a livin' is a lifestyle Exactly,

We said lovin' for a livin' We lovin' for a livin' Lovin' for a livin' is a lifestyle It's a lifestyle no matter what Oh yeah! It's a lifestyle They use it for shows Mommy is, I like her commercials because they're good and they're about God She is great She's here on a thousand and a million dollars That's what